MARK BRUNELL, FRED TAYLOR, GI
JIMMY SMITH, KEENAN MCCARDELL, KYLE
BRADY, TONY BOSELLI, MAURICE WILLIAMS,
VINCE MANUWAI, CHRIS NAEOLE, BRAD
MEESTER, PAUL SPICER, TONY BRACKENS,
JOHN HENDERSON, MARCUS STROUD, MIKE
PETERSON, KEVIN HARDY, AKIN AYODELE,
RASHEAN MATHIS, FERNANDO BRYANT,
DONOVIN DARIUS,
CARNELL LAKE,
JOSH SCOBEE, BRYAN BARKER, MARK
BRUNELL, FRED TAYLOR, GREG JONES,
JIMMY SMITH, KEENAN MCCARDELL,
KYLE BRADY, TONY BOSELLI, MAURICE
WILLIAMS, VINCE MANUWAI, CHRIS

THE STORY OF THE JACKSONVILLE JAGUARS

THE STORY OF THE JACKSONVILLE JAGUARS

BY JIM WHITING
CREATIVE EDUCATION / CREATIVE PAPERBACKS

Published by Creative Education and Creative Paperbacks
P.O. Box 227, Mankato, Minnesota 56002
Creative Education and Creative Paperbacks are imprints of The Creative Company
www.thecreativecompany.us

Design and production by Blue Design (www.bluedes.com)
Art direction by Rita Marshall
Printed in China

Photographs by AP Images (Associated Press), Getty Images (Julio Aguilar/Stringer, Doug Benc, John Biever/SI, Neil Brake/AFP, Stephen Dunn, Bill Frakes/SI, Larry French, Chris Graythen, Sam Greenwood, Otto Greule Jr./Allsport, Simeone Huber, Allen Kee/NFL, Andy Lyons, Andy Lyons/Allsport, David Maxwell/AFP, Al Messerschmidt, Don Juan Moore, Eliot J. Schechter, Jamie Squire, Robert Sullivan/AFP, Joe Traver/Time & Life Pictures, Chris Trotman)

Copyright © 2020 Creative Education, Creative Paperbacks
International copyright reserved in all countries. No part of this book may be reproduced in any form without written permission from the publisher.

Names: Whiting, Jim, author.
Title: The Story of the Jacksonville Jaguars / Jim Whiting.
Series: NFL Today.
Includes index.
Summary: This high-interest history of the National Football League's Jacksonville Jaguars highlights memorable games, summarizes seasonal triumphs and defeats, and features standout players such as Fred Taylor.
Identifiers: LCCN 2018035584 / ISBN 978-1-64026-144-0 (hardcover) / ISBN 978-1-62832-707-6 (pbk) / ISBN 978-1-64000-262-3 (ebook)
Subjects: LCSH: Jacksonville Jaguars (Football team)—History—Juvenile literature.
Classification: LCC GV956.J33 W55 2019 / DDC 796.332/640975912—dc23

First Edition HC 9 8 7 6 5 4 3 2 1
First Edition PBK 9 8 7 6 5 4 3 2 1

COVER: JALEN RAMSEY
PAGE 2: T.J. YELDON
PAGES 6–7: BRIAN WITHERSPOON

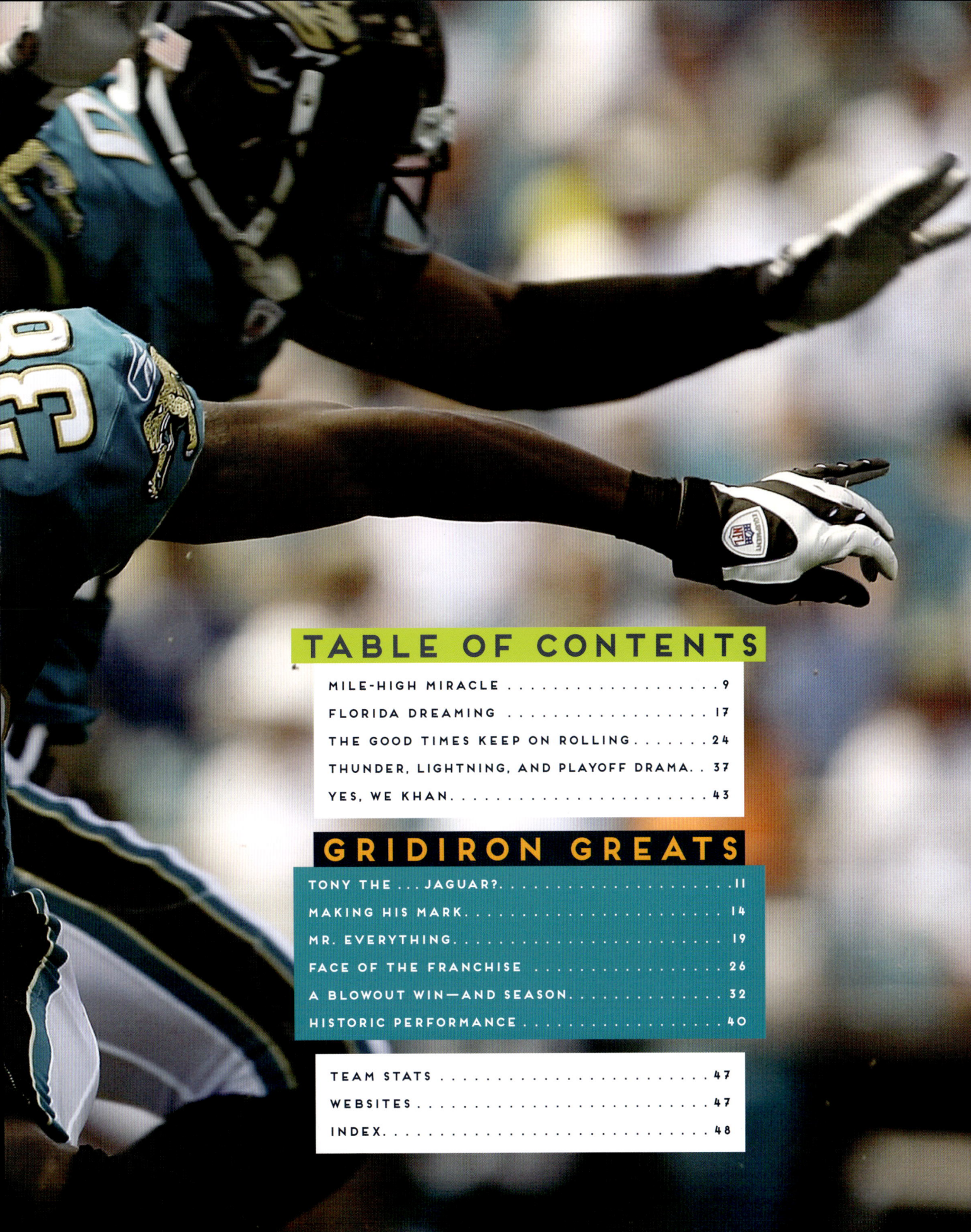

TABLE OF CONTENTS

MILE-HIGH MIRACLE	9
FLORIDA DREAMING	17
THE GOOD TIMES KEEP ON ROLLING	24
THUNDER, LIGHTNING, AND PLAYOFF DRAMA	37
YES, WE KHAN	43

GRIDIRON GREATS

TONY THE . . . JAGUAR?	11
MAKING HIS MARK	14
MR. EVERYTHING	19
FACE OF THE FRANCHISE	26
A BLOWOUT WIN—AND SEASON	32
HISTORIC PERFORMANCE	40

TEAM STATS	47
WEBSITES	47
INDEX	48

RUNNING BACK NATRONE MEANS

MILE-HIGH MIRACLE

Expansion teams in the National Football League (NFL) usually need several seasons before they can compete with other teams. The Jacksonville Jaguars began play in 1995. The team lived up (or down) to this expectation. It won just four games. The following season started out a bit better. The Jaguars won 4 of their first 11 games. Then they caught fire. They won their next five games. In the season's final game, they beat the Atlanta Falcons by two points. With a 9–7 mark, Jacksonville slipped into the playoffs. The Jaguars traveled to New York. They played the Buffalo Bills in the Wild Card round. They overcame a seven-point deficit in the fourth quarter. The Jaguars stunned the Bills. They won 30–27.

JACKSONVILLE JAGUARS

LEFT: RUNNING BACK JAMES STEWART

Then the Jaguars went to Denver. They faced the Broncos. Denver's 13–3 mark was the best in the American Football Conference (AFC) that year. Denver was favored to win. A local sports columnist suggested that Jacksonville was not a worthy opponent. "How do you get worked up to play somebody called Jacksonville with a bunch of nobodies?" he wrote. "Jacksonville? Is that a semi-pro team or a theme park?... Who do these upstart Jagwads think they are, anyway, coming to Mile High Stadium, where the Broncos haven't lost this season and only once ever in the playoffs?"

Denver scored two touchdowns in the first quarter. Its defense kept the Jaguars from getting a single first down. Then a funny thing happened: Jacksonville adjusted. The Jaguars scored two field goals and a touchdown in the second quarter. They clamped down on the Broncos' offense. Then came one of the greatest plays in Jacksonville history. The ball was at midfield. Quarterback Mark Brunell dropped back to pass. He was nearly sacked. But he squirmed away. He scrambled to Denver's 21-yard

TONY BOSELLI
LEFT TACKLE

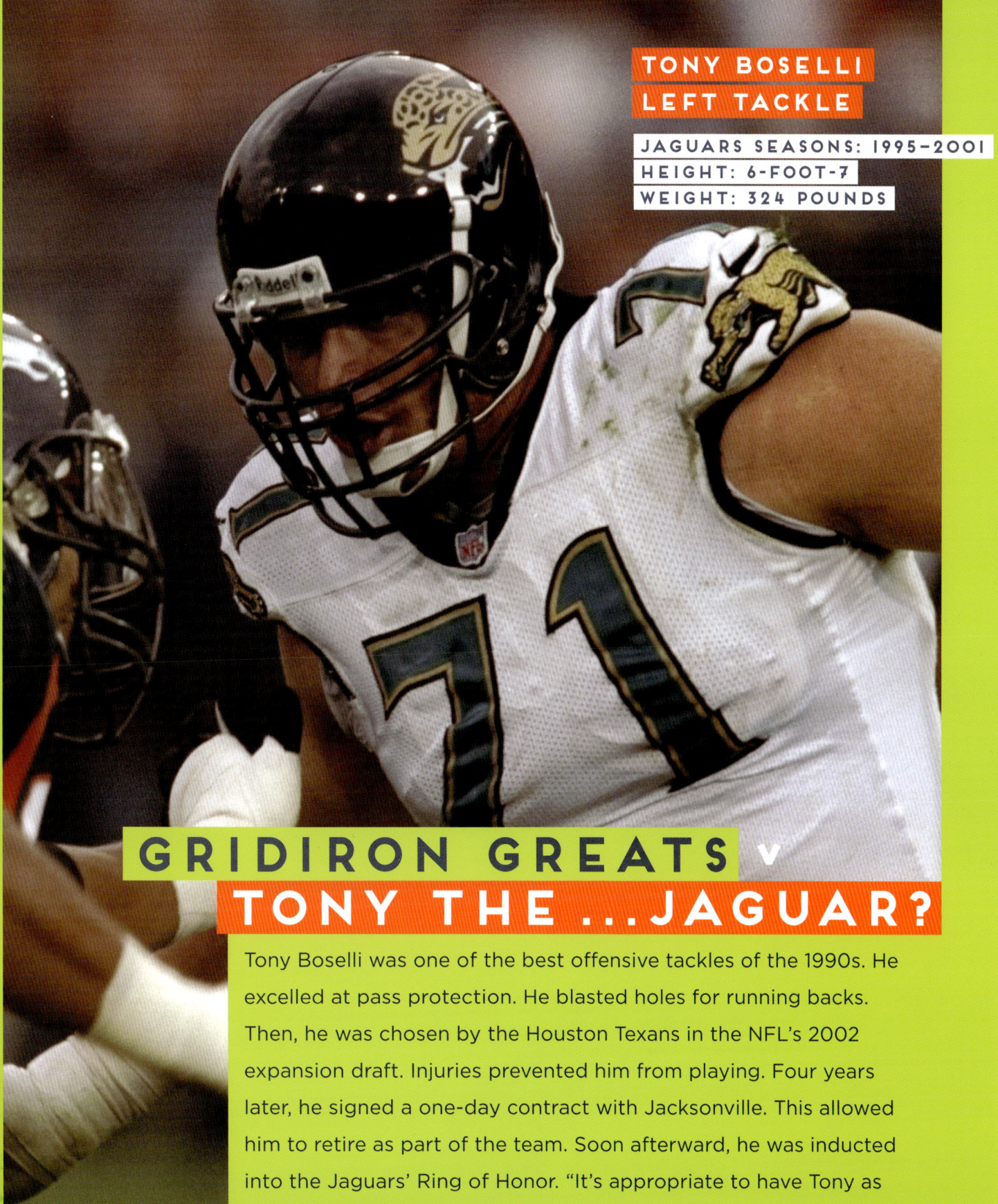

JAGUARS SEASONS: 1995–2001
HEIGHT: 6-FOOT-7
WEIGHT: 324 POUNDS

GRIDIRON GREATS
TONY THE...JAGUAR?

Tony Boselli was one of the best offensive tackles of the 1990s. He excelled at pass protection. He blasted holes for running backs. Then, he was chosen by the Houston Texans in the NFL's 2002 expansion draft. Injuries prevented him from playing. Four years later, he signed a one-day contract with Jacksonville. This allowed him to retire as part of the team. Soon afterward, he was inducted into the Jaguars' Ring of Honor. "It's appropriate to have Tony as the first member of the Ring of Honor as one of the all-time great Jaguars," said team owner Wayne Weaver.

MARK BRUNELL

"HE MADE HUGE PLAYS ALL DAY. YOU DON'T SEE A LOT OF GUYS WHO CAN MAKE THINGS HAPPEN LIKE HE CAN."

—JOHN ELWAY ON MARK BRUNELL

line. This play set up another touchdown. Jacksonville won, 30–27. "He made huge plays all day," Denver quarterback John Elway said about Brunell. "You don't see a lot of guys who can make things happen like he can."

The game became known as the "Mile-High Miracle." It has been called one of the greatest upsets in NFL history. A week after the "miracle," the Jaguars played the New England Patriots. The winner would be the AFC champion. That team would go to the Super Bowl. The Jaguars trailed by just a touchdown late in the fourth quarter. However, a Jacksonville fumble led to a 20–6 loss. But Jacksonville's ability to make it so far served notice: A new breed of cat was prowling in Florida.

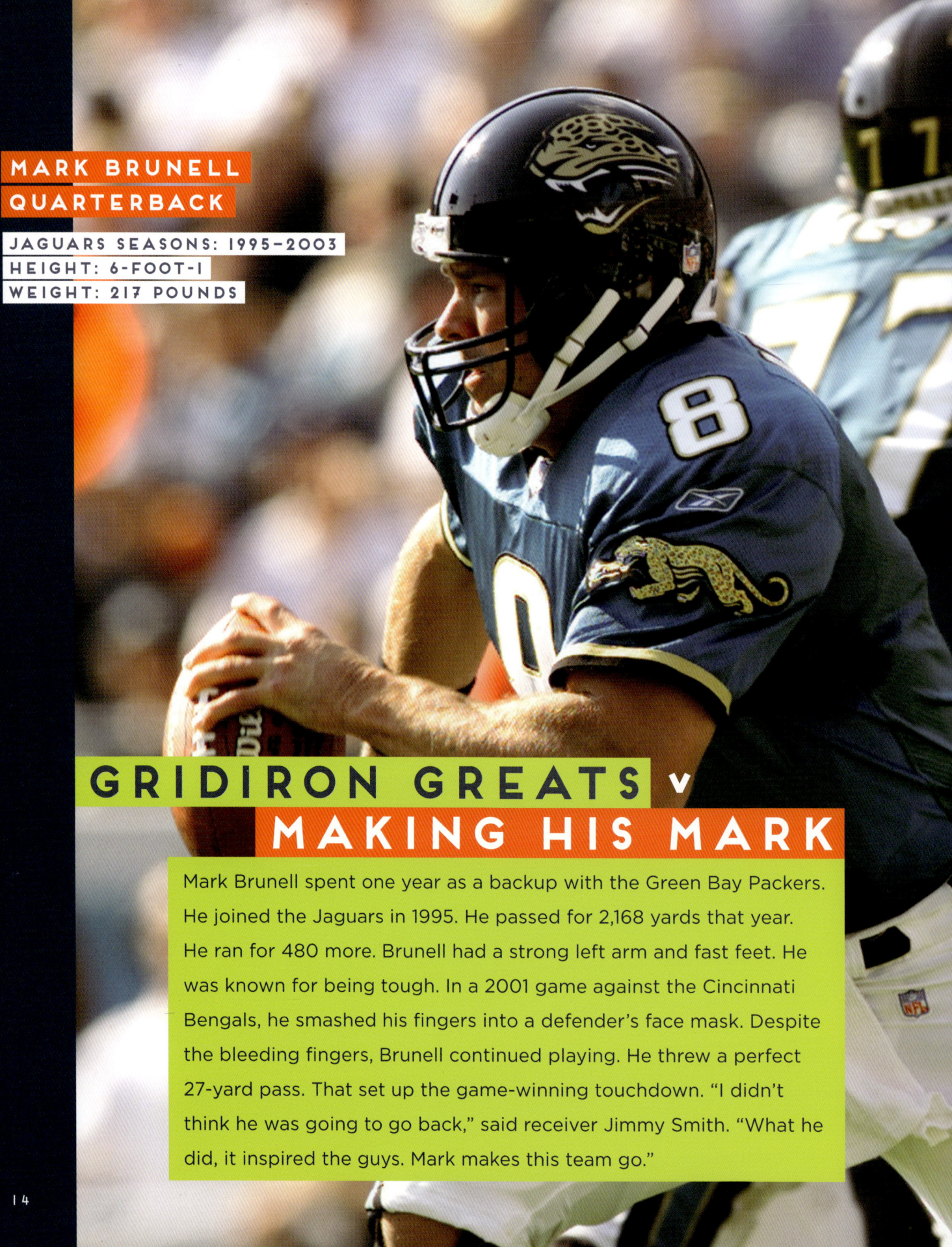

MARK BRUNELL
QUARTERBACK

JAGUARS SEASONS: 1995–2003
HEIGHT: 6-FOOT-1
WEIGHT: 217 POUNDS

GRIDIRON GREATS
MAKING HIS MARK

Mark Brunell spent one year as a backup with the Green Bay Packers. He joined the Jaguars in 1995. He passed for 2,168 yards that year. He ran for 480 more. Brunell had a strong left arm and fast feet. He was known for being tough. In a 2001 game against the Cincinnati Bengals, he smashed his fingers into a defender's face mask. Despite the bleeding fingers, Brunell continued playing. He threw a perfect 27-yard pass. That set up the game-winning touchdown. "I didn't think he was going to go back," said receiver Jimmy Smith. "What he did, it inspired the guys. Mark makes this team go."

FLORIDA DREAMING

Despite its large size and population, Jacksonville had no major professional sports franchise into the early 1990s. The city especially wanted an NFL team. It had already been home to three short-lived teams in lower football leagues. It had tried and failed to attract the Baltimore Colts and Houston Oilers when those teams decided to move. So the city was thrilled in 1993 when the NFL announced it was going to add two teams to the league.

In August 1989, a group called Touchdown Jacksonville had formed. Its goal was to prove that Jacksonville could support a team. The prospective owners held a team-

JACKSONVILLE JAGUARS

36
36 CAREER SACKS

134
134 GAMES PLAYED

KEVIN HARDY
LINEBACKER

JAGUARS SEASONS: 1996–2001
HEIGHT: 6-FOOT-4
WEIGHT: 259 POUNDS

GRIDIRON GREATS
MR. EVERYTHING

Kevin Hardy was the second overall choice in the 1996 NFL Draft. He notched 64 tackles and 5.5 sacks in his first year. He helped the Jaguars to their first playoff appearance. "He's done everything you could ask of a rookie to do," said defensive end Jeff Lageman. "Rarely do you find a rookie who can step in and make a difference." Hardy became a one-man wrecking crew. He could blitz the quarterback. He could also stuff the run. "As a linebacker, you've got to be involved in every phase of the game," Hardy said. "It's not just tackles, and it's not just interceptions. It's everything."

JACKSONVILLE JAGUARS

19

naming contest before they even knew if they'd have a club. Jaguars, the stealthy and muscular big cats of the Americas, was the most popular suggestion. Jaguars aren't native to Florida. But the Jacksonville Zoo features a large exhibit devoted to the animals. The group's work paid off. The NFL awarded one new franchise to Charlotte, North Carolina. Jacksonville received the other. Both would begin play in 1995.

In February 1995, the NFL held an expansion draft. Jacksonville and Carolina selected players from existing teams. The Jaguars chose veteran quarterback Steve Beuerlein to lead the team. They added explosive wide receiver Jimmy Smith. They traded for Brunell. He was a young, left-handed quarterback. Brunell was known for his quick feet. Two months later, the Jaguars participated in the regular NFL Draft. With their first pick, they took offensive tackle Tony Boselli.

On September 3, 1995, more than 72,000 fans packed Jacksonville Municipal Stadium. They eagerly watched their team take the field for the first time. The Jaguars lost the game to the Houston Oilers. Then they lost the next three. In their fifth game, the Jaguars faced the Oilers again. Beuerlein struggled. Brunell stepped in for him in the fourth quarter. Jacksonville trailed, 16–10. Brunell rallied the team. He threw a 15-yard touchdown pass to wide receiver Desmond Howard. Kicker Mike Hollis nailed the extra point. The Jaguars captured their first win! One week later, they won their first home game. They upset the Pittsburgh Steelers, 20–16.

NATRONE MEANS

> "I WAS EXCITED ABOUT MARK'S ATHLETICISM, HIS TOUGHNESS, HIS ABILITY TO MOVE IN THE POCKET, AND HIS ARM STRENGTH."
>
> —COACH TOM COUGHLIN ON BRUNELL

Brunell became one of the AFC's most exciting quarterbacks. "I studied players throughout the 1994 season, and I was excited about Mark's athleticism, his toughness, his ability to move in the pocket, and his arm strength," coach Tom Coughlin said. "I just felt like this would be the guy that we would want to lead our team." Defensively, the team added bite in the 1996 NFL Draft. The Jaguars took hard-hitting linebacker Kevin Hardy. As the season drew near, the Jaguars and their fans were dreaming big. But no one expected the dream to come true so quickly. Their trip ended just one game short of the Super Bowl. "[People] around the nation didn't know who we are. But they know now," said Hollis.

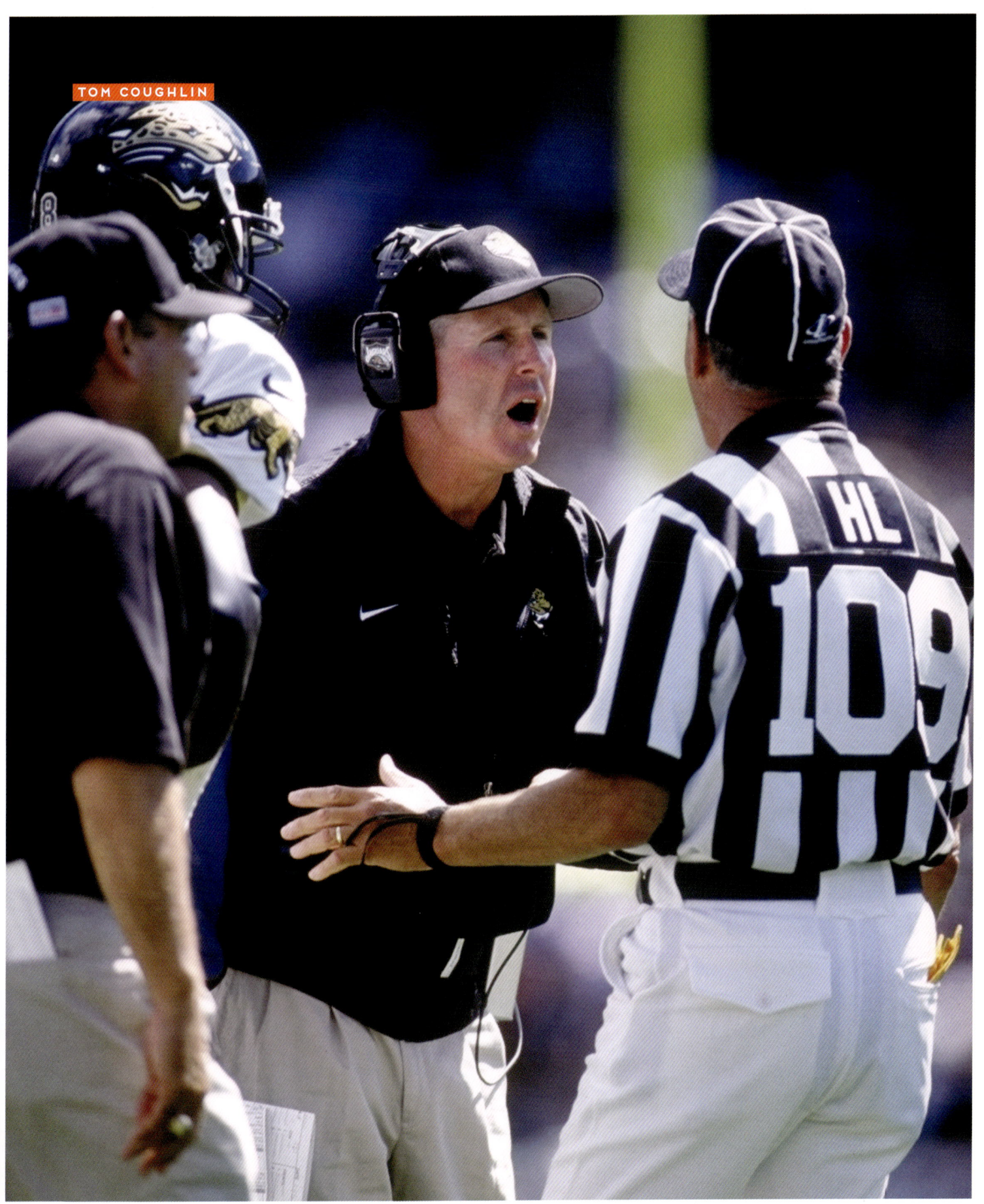
TOM COUGHLIN

JACKSONVILLE JAGUARS

THE GOOD TIMES KEEP ON ROLLING

WIDE RECEIVER KEENAN MCCARDELL

The Jaguars began the 1997 season determined to prove that 1996 hadn't been a fluke. Unfortunately, Brunell suffered a knee injury before the season. His backups managed to guide the team to a 2–0 start. Then Brunell returned. The Jags continued to roll. Keenan McCardell and Smith each posted more than 1,000 receiving yards during the season. The pair became known as "Thunder and Lightning." McCardell was "Thunder." He ran routes through the dangerous, linebacker-patrolled middle of the field. Smith was "Lightning" because of his speed.

GRIDIRON GREATS
FACE OF THE FRANCHISE

Fred Taylor was a Jaguar for more than a decade. He was the face of the franchise. Against the Indianapolis Colts in 2006, Taylor broke loose on the first play from scrimmage. He ran for 74 yards. In the second quarter, he made a spin move. He slipped between two defenders. They tackled each other. "We're not sure where Fred is going to run, but we just [block] our guys and let him go where he wants with the ball," said Jaguars offensive tackle Zach Wiegert. "It's a great feeling blocking for a guy like that, because you know he's going to make you look good."

**FRED TAYLOR
RUNNING BACK**

JAGUARS SEASONS: 1998–2008
HEIGHT: 6-FOOT-1
WEIGHT: 234 POUNDS

JACKSONVILLE JAGUARS

FRED TAYLOR

Running back James Stewart also earned a spot in the record books. He scored five touchdowns in a victory over the Philadelphia Eagles. He was only the ninth player in NFL history to accomplish this feat. The Jaguars finished the year 11–5. They returned to the playoffs. Jacksonville faced Denver in the first round. The Broncos took revenge for their defeat the previous year. They routed the Jaguars, 42–17.

In 1998, the Jaguars won their first five games. Then, injuries to Brunell and Stewart threatened to derail the season. Luckily, rookie running back Fred Taylor ignited the offense. On his very first carry, he raced 52 yards for

28

1998 AFC WILD CARD PLAYOFF

a touchdown. "Fred gives us an added dimension we've never had before," said tight end Rich Griffith. "When he gets going, we're hard to stop." Jacksonville went 11–5 again. This year, that record made them the AFC Central Division champions. In the first round of the playoffs, Taylor tore through the Patriots' defense. He rushed 162 yards. The Jags won, 25–10. But, a week later, they fell to the New York Jets.

TONY BOSELLI

DIVISIONAL ROUND

JAGUARS VS. MIAMI DOLPHINS
JACKSONVILLE, FLORIDA
JANUARY 15, 2000

GRIDIRON GREATS v
A BLOWOUT WIN—AND SEASON

The Jaguars enjoyed their greatest season in 1999. They finished the regular season 14-2. They were division champions for the second year in a row. But their most spectacular win occurred in the playoffs. They faced the Miami Dolphins. Before the game, skeptics doubted the Jaguars. None of Jacksonville's victories had come against teams with winning records. But Jacksonville led at halftime, 41-7. The final score was 62-7. The Jaguars racked up 520 yards of offense. They forced seven Miami turnovers. In addition, they held the Dolphins to a mere 131 yards of offense. "It was a great day for the Jaguars," said coach Tom Coughlin. "Our stadium was rocking and rolling today."

JACKSONVILLE JAGUARS

TIGHT END KYLE BRADY

The Jaguars were hungrier than ever in 1999. Their defense was the NFL's toughest. They allowed just 13.6 points per game. Defensive end Tony Brackens and cornerback Aaron Beasley were particularly disruptive. The pair tallied 13.5 sacks and 8 interceptions. Meanwhile, the offense held its own. Stewart and Taylor pounded the ball for 19 touchdowns. Smith recorded a career-high 116 receptions for 1,636 yards. These efforts led to a stunning 14–2 record. The team repeated as division champs. In the postseason, the Jaguars looked unstoppable. They crushed the Miami Dolphins 62–7. For the second time in their short history, the Jaguars were just one win away from the Super Bowl. But the Tennessee Titans beat them in the AFC Championship Game.

RUNNING BACK STACEY MACK

THUNDER, LIGHTNING, AND PLAYOFF DRAMA

As the saying goes, all good things must come to an end. In 2000, Taylor set a team rushing record with 1,399 yards. Smith and McCardell each posted more than 1,200 receiving yards. Smith cemented his status as one of the league's best wide receivers. In a game against the Baltimore Ravens, he caught 15 passes for 291 yards. But the Jaguars slipped to 7–9. The next year, they started with two wins. They lost eight of their next nine games. A modest three-game winning streak added some respectability to the season. They finished at 6–10.

Facing salary cap limits in 2002, the Jaguars said goodbye to Boselli and McCardell. The team went 6–10 again. It started the following season

LEFT: DEFENSIVE END REGGIE HAYWARD

with four losses. Even worse, Brunell suffered an elbow injury. Rookie quarterback Byron Leftwich took his place. Brunell eventually healed. But Leftwich remained the starter. The Jaguars finished with just five wins. Leftwich led the Jaguars to a 3–0 start in 2004. "Good teams find a way to win, and we want to become a good team," said coach Jack Del Rio. Another sign of a good team is the ability to win close games. Many of the Jaguars' victories that season were by narrow margins. But their 9–7 record wasn't quite good enough to reach the playoffs.

Leftwich was steadily improving. The Jaguars hoped he would lead the 2005 squad into the playoffs. The team roared to a strong start. It won 8 of its first 11 games. But in a matchup against the Arizona Cardinals, Leftwich broke his ankle. Backup quarterback David Garrard stepped up. The Jaguars finished with an impressive 12–4 record. But New England crushed them in the playoffs.

In 2006, the offense got a boost from rookie running back Maurice Jones-Drew. "MoJo" was just 5-foot-8. He was built like a bowling ball. He had surprising speed and power. Despite their strengths, the Jaguars finished at 8–8. In 2007, Jacksonville went 11–5. It earned a spot in the AFC Wild Card game. The Jaguars nearly blew a 28–10 lead against the Steelers. A last-minute field goal saved them. The Jaguars won, 31–29. Next, they faced the Patriots. New England had gone undefeated in the regular season. The Patriots continued their winning streak. They beat the Jaguars, 31–20. Jacksonville struggled through the next four seasons. The 2011 team had an especially weak offense. It averaged just 15.2 points a game. That was a team low.

BYRON LEFTWICH

WEEK 8

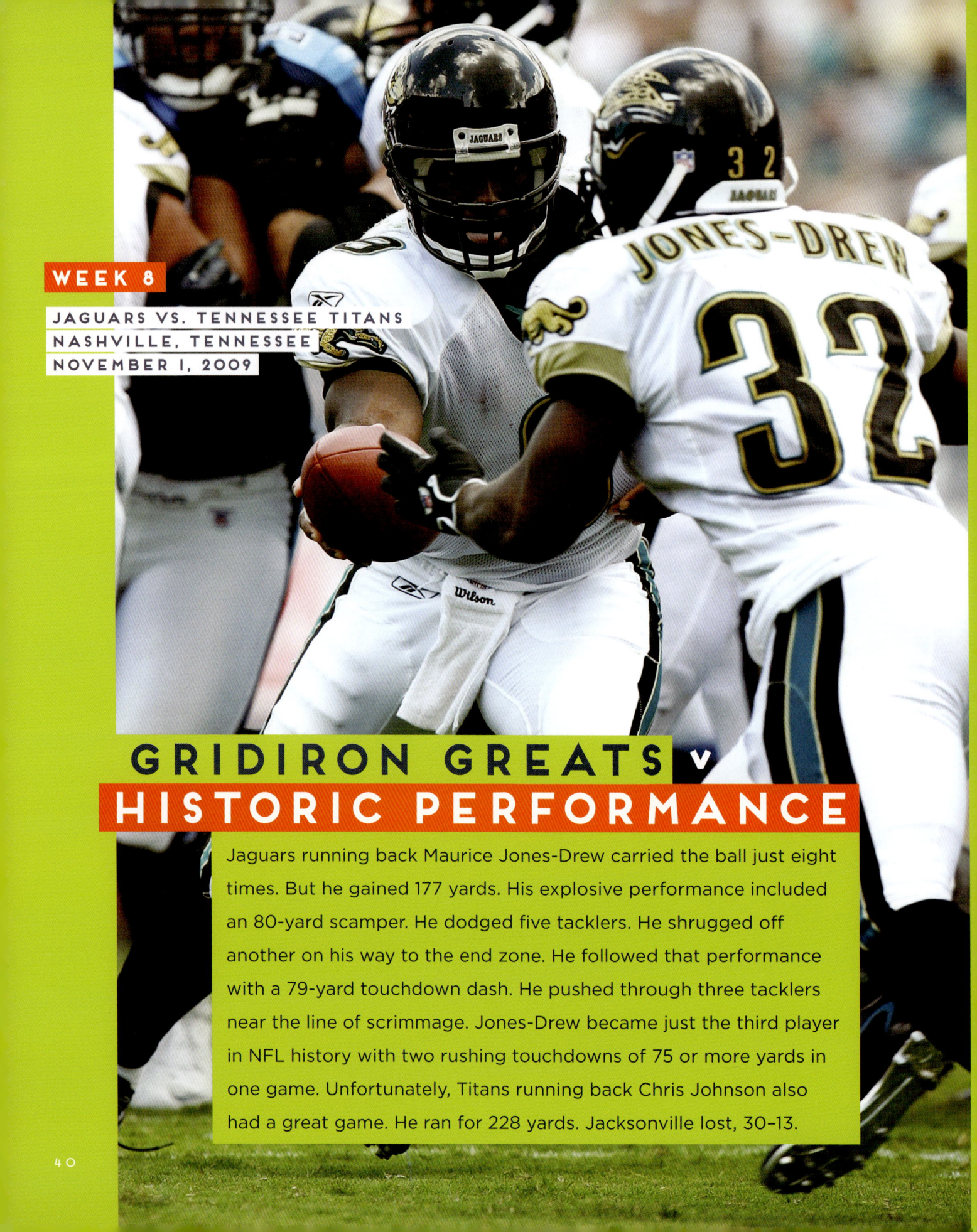

JAGUARS VS. TENNESSEE TITANS
NASHVILLE, TENNESSEE
NOVEMBER 1, 2009

GRIDIRON GREATS
HISTORIC PERFORMANCE

Jaguars running back Maurice Jones-Drew carried the ball just eight times. But he gained 177 yards. His explosive performance included an 80-yard scamper. He dodged five tacklers. He shrugged off another on his way to the end zone. He followed that performance with a 79-yard touchdown dash. He pushed through three tacklers near the line of scrimmage. Jones-Drew became just the third player in NFL history with two rushing touchdowns of 75 or more yards in one game. Unfortunately, Titans running back Chris Johnson also had a great game. He ran for 228 yards. Jacksonville lost, 30–13.

16

16 JAGUARS RUSHING ATTEMPTS

217

217 JAGUARS RUSHING YARDS

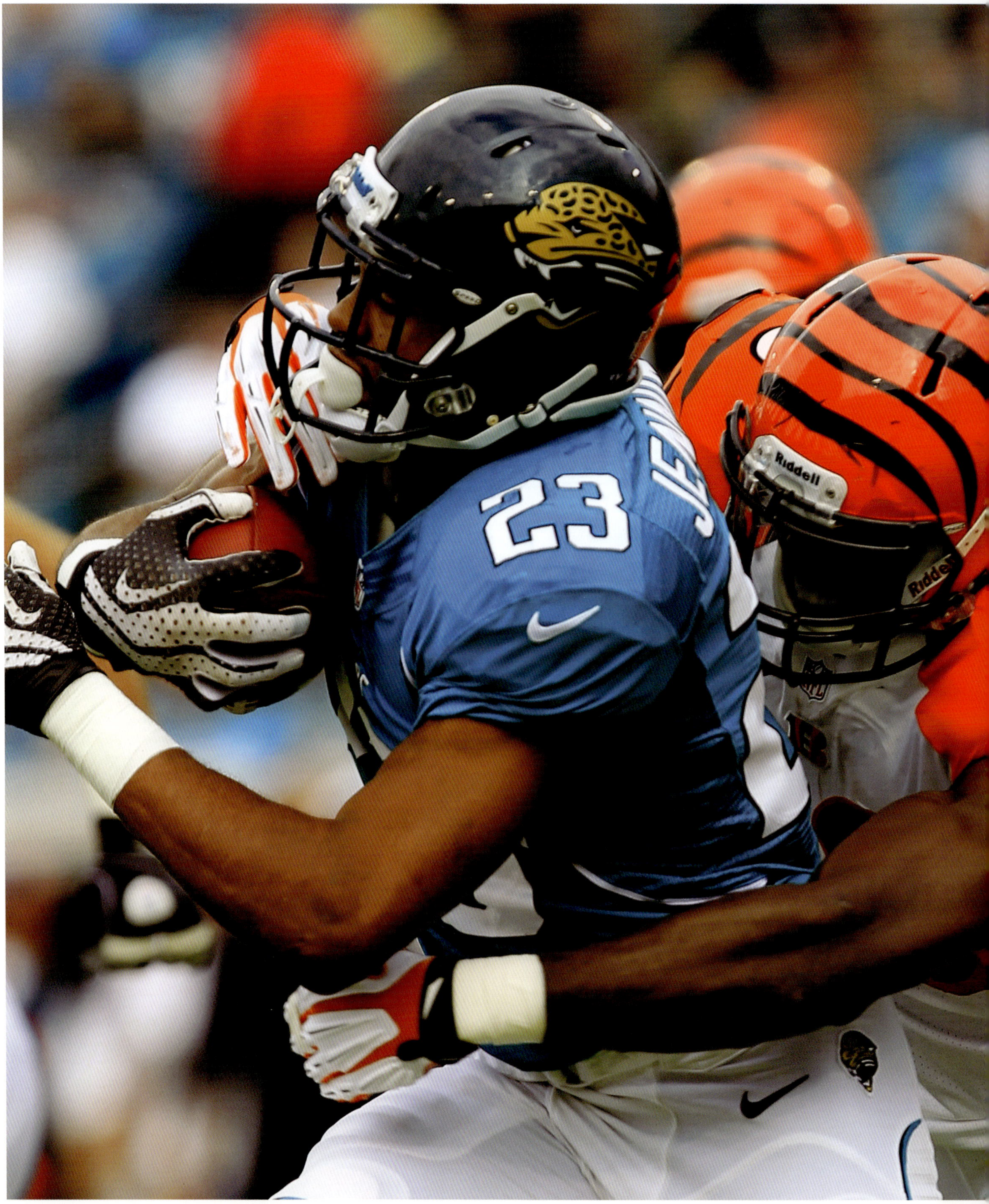
23
Riddell

RUNNING BACK RASHAD JENNINGS

YES, WE KHAN

Businessman Shahid Khan bought the Jaguars in 2012. His main concern was boosting the team's passing attack. To do that, he hired former Falcons offensive coordinator Mike Mularkey as coach. "This is a team that is very close to making things happen, and I'm here to make sure it does happen," said Mularkey. Unfortunately, nothing happened. Jacksonville fell to 2–14 that year. It was the worst record in team history. Mularkey was fired. In 2013, the Jaguars won just four games. The next year, the team drafted quarterback Blake Bortles. He had some

JACKSONVILLE JAGUARS

JACKSONVILLE JAGUARS

impressive games. But the team continued to struggle. Jacksonville won just three games in 2014. It posted a mark of 5–11 the following year. Despite the team's poor record, other NFL players recognized that Bortles could become something special. They named him as number 56 in their annual compilation of the NFL Top 100 Players after the 2015 season. But Bortles was limited by injuries in 2016. After a 2–3 start, Jacksonville lost nine games in a row. It ended the season at 3–13.

The Jaguars matched their 2016 win total in Week 5 of the 2017 season. They topped the Steelers in a convincing victory. By the end of the season, the team had compiled a 10–6 record. It was back in the playoffs for the first time in 10 years! One key to its success was veteran defensive tackle Calais Campbell. He had a team-record four sacks in the 29–7 season-opening win over the Houston Texans. He added 10.5 more during the year. That set a new team single-season record.

Jacksonville beat Buffalo in the Wild Card round. Then the team traveled to Pittsburgh. It upset the Steelers in a 45–42 shootout. The Jaguars faced the Patriots with a Super Bowl berth on the line. Jacksonville held a 10-point lead in the fourth quarter. But Patriots quarterback Tom Brady engineered a late-game comeback. New England won by four. Despite the loss, Khan appreciated his team's turnaround. "I've been through life when I was a

LEFT: WIDE RECEIVER JUSTIN BLACKMON

BLAKE BORTLES

RUNNING BACK LEONARD FOURNETTE

laughingstock, whatever business I was in—auto parts, what have you—and then you have to stay with it, and success comes," he said. "It's a story of perseverance." The team would have to continue waiting for success, after its 5–11 finish in 2018.

The Touchdown Jacksonville group spent years on the hunt for an NFL franchise. Then, Jacksonville's cats pounced into the football world. In the team's first five seasons, it made the playoffs four times and reached two AFC Championship Games. The Jaguars of the past have stalked within striking distance of the Super Bowl. But the big cats remain hungry. A new generation is eager for the hunt that will end with an NFL title.

TEAM STATS

AFC DIVISION CHAMPIONS

1998, 1999, 2017

WEBSITES

JACKSONVILLE JAGUARS
https://www.jaguars.com/

NFL: JACKSONVILLE JAGUARS TEAM PAGE
http://www.nfl.com/teams/jacksonvillejaguars/profile?team=JAX

INDEX

JACKSONVILLE JAGUARS

AFC Championship Game 13, 34, 46
Beasley, Aaron 34
Beuerlein, Steve 21
Bortles, Blake 43, 44
Boselli, Tony 11, 21, 37
Brackens, Tony 34
Brunell, Mark 10, 13, 14, 21, 22, 24, 38
Campbell, Calais 44
Coughlin, Tom 22, 32
Del Rio, Jack 38
division championships 31, 32, 34
Garrard, David 38

Griffith, Rich 31
Hardy, Kevin 19, 22
Hollis, Mike 21, 22
Howard, Desmond 21
Jacksonville Municipal Stadium 21
Jaguars name 21
Jones-Drew, Maurice 38, 40
Khan, Shahid 43, 44
Lageman, Jeff 19
Leftwich, Byron 38
McCardell, Keenan 24, 37
"Mile-High Miracle" 13
Mularkey, Mark 43
NFL Draft 19, 21, 22

playoffs 9, 19, 28, 31, 32, 38, 44, 46
Ring of Honor 11
Smith, Jimmy 14, 21, 24, 34, 37
Stewart, James 28, 34
Taylor, Fred 26, 28, 31, 34, 37
team records 37, 44
Touchdown Jacksonville 17, 46
Weaver, Wayne 11
Wiegert, Zach 26

DEFENSE VS. TITANS 2008